The Happiest Golfer

Stories, Insight, and Inspiration to Make You Happier on and off the Course

by Bryan Skavnak

Prologue

Why write about happiness?

There was a story that I heard in college about a philosophy class. The final exam was 50% of the grade. And the final exam only had one question.

Why do you believe in God?

Within about 10 seconds of receiving the exam, one of the students got up, handed it to the professor, and left the room.

Everyone else was stunned. How could someone be done so fast? What could he have written that could possible have counted as an answer?

The grade was posted the next day and the kid got an A.

His answer to the final exam question: Why not?

Everyone has their own perspective. That was his.

So, why not write about happiness?

I want to be happier and you want to be happier.

I believe that if you want to be happy, then you can be happy. And if you know what makes you happy, then you can always be happy.

On the golf course and in life, I know what makes me happy and what makes me turn into a bizarro version of myself.

And I want to share, in hopes that it will help you.

My way of sharing happiness is through storytelling.

For me, stories are a way to teach. And the best thing about stories is that people learn different things from them.

Some are funny, some are serious, some may seem random, but hopefully every one of them has a lesson.

I write like I read...in little chunks. Maybe it's adult onset ADD or maybe that's how my creative juices work. So, each story can be read on its own. But reading them together will put the theme together more clearly.

And, the entire book can be read in one sitting...depending on how long you like to sit.

This isn't a golf book that teaches technical aspects of the game. Some people have told me that this isn't even a golf book at all.

It's a life book with golf stories.

I'm lucky enough to be happy, and now I want to share what I learned with you.

Below are some things you need to know about me and this book before you start reading.

1. I operate a golf academy for kids and families.

2. I'm half serious, half sarcastic, half goofy, and not very good with fractions.

3. I reference my wife, Kim, and kids, Ethan and Ella in the book. Kim is a photographer. Ethan loves trains. And Ella will bite your hand off if you have frosting in it.

4. There is a central theme, but the book is broken into small segments and stories, so if you're like me and lack focus, then you can...I forgot what I was writing.

5. I talk about food a lot. I love food. And I will eat anything, except for sweet potatoes. Sweet potatoes are the devil's vomit.

6. I have 11 different colored belts, only two of which glow in the dark.

7. If you love Nickelback, you will hate this book.

8. I won an award in a high school class for best journal writing. I was the first guy to win it. Not sure what that means.

9. There are some pop culture references made that you may not understand. It's okay. We can't all be as culturally aware as Abed Nadir. That's why Al Gore invented Google.

10. I am a good listener, unless apparently, I am married to you.

11. I eat Jolly Rancher suckers like some people drink water.

12. The best way to read this is with a chicken wing in one hand, a beer in the other, and a cookie in the other. Darn that fraction thing.

13. When it comes to humor, I'm not Jay Leno, Jeff Dunham, or Larry the Cable Guy...so this thing has a chance of being funny.

Chapter 1

Time to Share

Ever since I was a little Bryan, I have enjoyed writing and being creative. I can't draw or paint, but if you ask my bro, we put on some of the best "variety" shows of the early 90's. And by variety, I mean, we sang MC Hammer songs and did the typewriter.

When I was in grade school, I enjoyed the writing projects and the stories that we had to tell. I loved giving speeches.

When I got to college, one class project was to operate a fictitious baking company...I was in charge of writing the completely made up monthly newsletter. Our "company" softball team was Two Strikes and No Balls. Discuss.

After college, I started a real business and used writing in different ways. I would write brief descriptions of golf classes. I'd write about pages on my site. But it didn't feel right. This new kind of business writing wasn't creative. It was too descriptive and didn't show my personality. It never felt genuinely me.

And my writing reflected that.

There was nothing for people to relate to. There was no human behind the company. It was advertising, not marketing.

It wasn't real.

My wife will tell you that I don't remember a lot of things, but I always remember this quote.

["If it looks good, you'll see it. If it sounds good, you'll hear it. If it's marketed right, you'll buy it. But... if it's real, you'll feel it."]
-Bob Ritchie (Google Bob Ritchie...you'll be surprised)

I think I was scared of the real.

I didn't know what would happen if I just put myself out there…if I wrote what I felt…if I focused on helping rather than selling.

I was scared that people would go somewhere else if I wrote on a personal level.

And it was this fear that prevented me from showing what I really could do.

Then my mom died.

Everyone has that sink or swim moment.

That time in your life where you show what you're made of.

You can feel sorry for yourself. You can give up. You can believe that the world is against you.

Or you can fight. You can make a negative into a positive. You can be resilient. You can use your story to help others.

My sink or swim moment happened when my mom died.

There are a lot of negatives to be had when a 62 year old woman dies of cancer only 7 months after the diagnosis.

There were many people who were angry. There were many people who said it was unfair.

Thank God, mom didn't see those people.

She was a saint. She was selfless, caring, loving, goofy, supportive, and happy. Man, was she happy.

Throughout the whole ordeal, I was never once angry. I still am not.

Death sucks. But things get better.

During those last two days at the hospital with her, we had some great moments. We talked about funny and touching memories with my dad, brother, wife, aunts and uncles.

We were sad. But we were happy too.

And it hit me when we were in the hospital.

Life is about stories. Life is about memories. Life is about the experience.

And stories and memories and experiences can help other people.

I always have had this dream about winning the lottery. I've had a lot of dreams about secret forts and that Stay Puft dude from Ghostbusters too, but I digress.

I wanted to win the lottery, live modestly, and then take care of the people around me. In short, I wanted to win a lot of money, so I could give a lot of money away.

I'd help my family, my friends, college buddies, waitresses, random guys on the street. Just about everyone.

Sitting in the hospital watching my mom die, I realized something.

The lottery has nothing to do with money.

I had already won the lottery.

I was living the dream. I had a loving wife, two awesomely fun kids, a supportive family, and the dream job.

I teach golf.

Not only do I teach golf. But I teach golf to kids and families.

I've taught golf to kids and families for over 13 years now. Not only do I show them how to play the game, but I show them things that will help them with their lives as well; manners, respect, self confidence, laughter, generosity.

There are countless numbers of things that I have learned throughout my years of teaching, studying, and talking with kids that help them become good golfers. But more importantly...these things help them become good people.

So, I decided to give away my lottery.

I decided it's time to share my knowledge, my experience, my inspiration, and my humor with everyone.

I made the choice not to be scared anymore.

So, I wrote.

I wrote what I felt.

I wrote a letter about my mom and sent it to my list of students, parents, and followers. I titled this letter "Laughing and Crying," I shared the one major thing that my mom taught me. The one thing that can help every kid who takes lessons, every parent that raises children, every person who wants to be happy.

Perspective.

I still remember the day that I sent that letter out.

I figured one of two things was going to happen. Either people were going to relate to it and love it. Or people were going to wonder why the heck a golf pro was sending out an email like this and hang me by my clown feet.

After only a couple days, I had thousands of people read the letter.

I had hundreds and hundreds of responses from students, former students, and people I didn't even know.

I was blown away.

So, I kept writing. I kept sharing.

I wrote funny things. I wrote serious things. I wrote inspirational things. I wrote things that probably only made me laugh (that's what happens to a kid that grew up on Saturday Night Live).

But each one of these notes had a message...a simple formula of funny, story, lesson.

I kept getting more and more positive feedback.

So, I kept sharing. I kept telling stories.

Again, I realized something profound.

I have a message that I want to get out to the world.

I have a message of happiness and perspective. I have a message that golf and life intersect. I have a message of inspiration and hope and giving.

And, this message can be shared with others to help them. To show them that they can be happy. To show them that when life gives you lemons, don't make lemonade, open up a lemonade stand, and help other people. Give what you got.

Fear is just an excuse.

Everyone has something to share.

I'm hoping that my sharing makes you happier.

Chapter 2

The Secret I Learned at TGI Friday's

I have learned a lot at restaurants.

And if the law of averages works out, I know a lot.....because I eat a lot.

1. I've learned that Old Country Buffet considers 50 "Old."

2. I've learned that eating 4 plates of food and two steaks at the Treasure Island buffet will not only make your stomach hurt, but it will also make you pass out for a half hour in your hotel room.

3. I've learned that no matter how much you eat at a Chinese buffet, you are always hungry exactly two hours later.

4. I've learned that you can bring your mom and her two friends to Pizza Luce, be served by a waitress with piercings in things that I didn't even know could be

pierced, and not be kicked out as your mom orders a water with a lemon.

5. I've learned that you can convince the waitress that "the smaller the bill, the bigger the tip."

6. I've learned that "Hi, I'm ____, and I'll be taking care of you tonight" is waiter code for "I just started yesterday and am going to charge you extra for ranch."

7. I've learned that if you stand up from breakfast before a golf tournament, and hit your head on the corner of a tv, not only will your head bleed profusely, but you will have absolutely zero recollection of the round of golf you probably shouldn't have played.

8. I've learned that even on 20 screens, two of which are bigger than my car, Major League Soccer is still not fun to watch.

9. I've learned that "Would you like a refill on your fajitas?" is the greatest 8-word sentence ever uttered.

But the most important lesson I've ever learned at a restaurant happened with my dad.

Because it was the day he taught me the secret.

We had just finished up refereeing a very well played, hotly contested 7th grade girls basketball game (good, you can sense sarcasm), and we were headed some place to eat.

After every night of reffing, we'd go somewhere to eat and spend time together.

On this night, our choice was TGI Fridays.

The first few minutes usually went like this:

Dad: Wanna split some nachos?
Me: Yep.

Followed by:

Dad: Are you going to have ice cream?
Me: Yep.

Okay, it probably didn't go like that all the time, but man, I love nachos. And I think it's a law that you have to finish every meal with ice cream.

So on this night, as usual, we ate our food, told some jokes, and had a great time.

There were three guys in a booth behind us. Another guy noticed them on his walk in and stopped to say hi. You could tell from the onset that they hadn't seen each other in a long time.

Their conversation went on for a few minutes, but I noticed that something was off about it.

One guy asked the "new" guy how he was doing. New guy answered the question like this, "Great, I'm living in a really nice house, I'm driving this awesome car, and

I'm getting paid a lot at my job. You guys should come out to the club some day and I'll take you golfing."

The other guys chimed in with info on their cars, their houses, their club memberships.

New guy answered the question by telling the other guys everything he HAD. He told them about all his STUFF.

At our separate conversation in our booth things got serious. Not serious in the emotional sense or the Yahoo sense (insert obscure 1988 reference).

This was serious in the learning sense.

After hearing these guys brag for a while, my dad looked at me and said, "You know what. Life isn't about all the stuff. It isn't about getting all these things. It's about surrounding yourself with good people and taking care of the people around you."

Game. Set. Match.

I don't even know if my dad knew how important that was at the time. But it is the ONLY thing that is important. Because without good people around you, you have nothing. You have nobody to laugh with, you have nobody to cry with, you have nobody to share special moments with.

The good people are the ones that make you happy.

Don't try to impress people with all your stuff. If you really want to impress them, help them. Teach them. Show them that people are more important than stuff. Your friends are more important than your score. Your family is more important than trophy. The experience is more important than winning.

And good people attract other good people.

Be one of the good ones.

Chapter 3

Laughing and Crying

Something funny happens when you lose someone close to you.

You start to remember.

I don't remember to take out the garbage. I don't remember to pick up milk from the store. I even forgot my own birthday once.

But, when my mom died, I remembered everything.

Childhood memories, family memories…they all just jump back into your mind.

If you stop to realize it, you have a lot of good memories. And these good memories are good stories. You laughed, you cried, you smiled. You spent time with people you love.

With memories come learning experiences. You usually need to take a step back to understand what you had or what you learned. But it's always there.

One week after my mom died, I sent out this letter to my family, friends, and fans.

[I lost my number one fan last week.

After battling lymphoma for seven tough months, my mom died on Tuesday.

She was the happiest person you'd ever meet. She would talk your face off. When I was growing up, some people even thought that I was mute because I could never get a word in.

She was pro-family all the way...dinners together, holidays together, anything you could think of....together.

She started to learn how to golf because it was a fun family thing to do. She was never very good, but she had fun with it.

My mom was the one who asked religiously every time I came home, if I got a hole in one. She only forgot to ask once. And I had to remind her...because that's the day I got a hole in one.

My mom was the one who'd walk along with me and root me on during my playing days, even when she couldn't see where the ball went. I remember a time at a Monticello tournament, where I ripped two out of bounds, and she said, "Nice shot BR."

My mom was the one who would say to me, "Don't worry Bryan, I don't tell anyone you tried to teach me...you'll lose business if I do!"

You always learn a lot from people you're the closest to. Some things are specifically taught and others you just pick up along the way.

My mom taught me about manners, and generosity, and treating others kindly. She taught me how to play 500 (she was a rockstar at that game), how to make ice cream pie, and how to do laundry. She taught me how to pray, how to talk to others, and how to sing incorrect song lyrics. Seriously, I still don't know what a heebeejeebee is.

She taught me it's okay to laugh and it's okay to cry.

But the greatest gift my mom ever gave me was perspective.

It was the realization that you can be happy if you choose to be happy. It was the fact that no matter how bad you have it, someone else has it worse. It was not knowing all the answers, but always looking for ways to make things better. It was perpetual positivity.

There is no glass half empty or glass half full. There is just a glass, and you put what you want into it.

My mom was happy until the end. She never complained, never wondered why this happened to her, and through it all worried about how we were doing.

It takes a special person to stay positive through tough times. Although it takes a very special person to talk to a wrong number for 20 minutes (she had done that before too!).

I'll leave you with my favorite mom story ever. It was just between us two and I've never laughed so hard in my life. To my friends, it's simply known as Peanut Butter Chocolate Chip.

We were shopping at Brookdale in the winter. We parked near Sears and had to walk through it to get to the mall. On the way out, I saw someone who worked there that I knew, and didn't feel like talking to at the time. I looked at my mom and said, "Okay, how are we going to do this?" Without hesitation, my mom said, "We need code words." I almost lost it right there.

My mom saying, "we need code words" was the equivalent to me saying, "No thanks, I don't want any more cake." You never saw it coming.

So we came up with a plan.

I was going to weave through the store, Frogger-style, with my mom shouting "code words" when I should go left or right. In retrospect, I could have taken a different door out, but this was way more fun.

"Okay mom, what are the code words?"

"If you should go left, I'll say chocolate chip.

"And what if I need to go right?"

"Peanut butter."

So, the plan began.

I started walking through an aisle and all of a sudden heard my mom screaming, "Peanut butter!, Peanut butter!, Peanut butter!"

I went to the right and walked DIRECTLY in front of the person I did not want to talk to.

But I was okay, because he never saw me. He was too busy staring at this crazy woman yelling "Peanut butter" in the middle of Sears.

We got to the exit and we both stopped. We were laughing hysterically at this point. My mom looked at me and said, "Where were you going? I said peanut butter and you went chocolate chip."

"No. Peanut butter is right, chocolate chip is left."

By this time, people were staring at us because I think we were hyperventilating near the doors.

We walked out to the parking lot and I started going the wrong way. My mom looked at me and deadpanned, "Hey BR, the car is to the peanut butter."

Until the very end, my mom still thought peanut butter was to the left.

It's okay to laugh and it's okay to cry.

I hope you find your Peanut Butter Chocolate Chip. And remember, perspective is everything. Thanks Mom.]

These memories are what sustain us. They are what can keep us in good spirits, even when life tries to beat you down.

Look at things differently.

Find whatever seems to be bothering you or bringing you negativity, and find the positive.

Ask yourself one question.

What is good about this situation?

There is always something good. You just have to look for it.

Chapter 4

Choose to Be Better

I'm convinced that everyone would be a better golfer if they didn't have a head.

Because it's our own head that spews those toxic thoughts:

"You went in the water last time."
"Everyone is watching you."
"Don't screw up."
"You always miss this one."

I played golf once with a guy that said, "I haven't hit a bad drive in a while, so I'm probably due."

You don't hop in your car in the morning and think, "Well, I haven't run my car into that tree in a long time, so I'm probably due."

"I haven't chopped my finger off cutting vegetables for while, I'm probably due."

"You know what, I haven't crapped my pants in a while, I'm probably due."

Of course you're going to hit a bad shot if all you think about is bad shots. If you get up to a hole and only see the water and woods, there's a good chance your ball is tracking toward them.

Those thoughts invade our minds all the time.

And a lot of people seem to be okay with it.

"Oh, I always hit it there."
"I knew I was going to miss that."
"That's my normal game."
"I was waiting for that to happen."

Obstacles are inevitable. You can choose to look at them as a hassle or you can choose to be better.

Don't set yourself up for failure before you even try.

Don't be content with how you are or how people think you are.

If you don't like it, change it.

If you want something different, then create something different.

Quit undervaluing yourself.

Why are we always focused on the bad stuff? Why can't we be better than we think we are?

I have students that constantly say to me after every shot, "What was wrong with that one? or "What did I do wrong there?"

What!!?

What did I do wrong?

Why do you want to know what you did wrong all the time? So you can PREVENT yourself from doing something wrong again?

When I cook dinner for my family, which is usually the choice between fajitas or ice cream pie (I'm not exactly a culinary wiz), I don't ask my wife when we're eating, "So, what is it that you hate about this meal?"

You don't walk up the stairs trying NOT to fall down. You don't eat food trying NOT to stab yourself with your fork.

I've been teaching golf for 13 years. And in those 13 years, I can count on one hand how many people have answered this next question positively.

"How did you play?"

Almost every single person says that they didn't play well. Every single person says they could have done better. Every single person says they made mistakes.

Bravo. You're a golfer. And you're a person.

We all do dumb things. We all fail. We all fall down.

The difference is that happy people can get back up and do it a different way.

Happy people realize that it's okay to be wrong. They also realize that they can make the change.

Being a happy person doesn't start with anything on the outside. It starts with you.

It starts with a choice to be better.

What separates the happy people from the rest is this choice.

Unhappy people will say, "Okay, that's the way it is. I can't change it." Happy people say, "I'm making this better."

Unhappy people say, "I don't know how to do that." Happy people say, "I don't know how to do that, but I'm going to learn how."

When we first had Ethan (our oldest, but not goofiest), I was working long hours. I didn't have time to go out with friends. I didn't have time to do the things that I had liked to do before kids. I liked golfing with my dad. I liked going out with my bro. I liked going to see live music.

I knew in the back of my mind, that with this new family responsibility, my fun would have to stop (or at least slow down).

But I was selfish.

I didn't change.

I went out with my bro anyway. I went to shows anyway.

And I did the worst thing that I could have done.

I took my wife for granted.

I knew she'd be home with Ethan. I figured that if I worked outside the home, then she'd take care of things inside the home.

I was an idiot.

The only way that things would get better was if I was better. I couldn't go on doing the same things that I was doing and have a good balance. I couldn't think of me first. I had to change perspective.

Perspective jumps out at very pivotal moments in your life. But the cool thing is that you can choose your path. You can choose to be better or you can choose to maintain. Some people like maintaining. I'm not one of those people.

So, I chose to change.

Is it that easy to just choose?

I would argue, yes.

Because you realize quickly what is really important to you. Once you figure out what is important, the choice becomes clear.

But why don't we make this choice? Why don't we choose to be better and be different?

Fear.

We are scared to be vulnerable. We are scared to show our true selves. We are scared to admit we need to change. We are scared that what we can give isn't good enough. We are scared of the responsibility. We are scared to be different.

But when you look at that fear and realize that most of it is self projected, you'll be okay.

Everyone is scared.

Happy people realize that limiting fear is a way to become happier.

For me, family was more important than playing golf (and that's a tough thing for a golf pro to say.)

I don't go to as many shows as before, but I still go to some. And my kids know more lyrics to Dawes songs than Barney songs, so I think I'm doing all right.

This is one of my favorite quotes of all time:

[The greatest thing about tomorrow is I will be better than I am today. And that's how I look at my life. I will be better as a golfer, I will be better as a person, I will be better as a father, I will be a better husband, I will be better as a friend. That's the beauty of tomorrow. There is no such thing as a setback. The lessons I learn today I will apply tomorrow, and I will be better.]
(Google who said it....you'll be surprised)

I understand that my golf game can never be perfect. I understand that my life can never be perfect. But I always try to be better.

You can never beat golf, just like you can never beat life. It's always a work in progress. It's about the experience and what you learn along the way...because there can never be a perfect. And why would you want perfection anyway? Then there's nothing to work toward. Your goal should be to always be better.

Listen to people around you. Hear what they say and how they say it. Are they complaining? Are they placing blame? Are most of their words negative?

Be the opposite.

Give compliments. Accept responsibility. Work harder. Smile more.

You can always be better.

You just have to choose to be better.

Chapter 5

The Happiness Trifecta

I watch people.

Whoa, that sounds creepy. Let me try again.

I look at people.

Nope, still creepy.

I am aware of people.

Okay, that's a little better.

I am aware of people and their actions. I watch to see what they do to become happy and I see how that can apply to my life.

That is why I told the previous three stories. To make you aware of what I like to call The Happiness Trifecta. Happiness is already in front of you. And throughout the book, you'll learn this.

The Happiness Trifecta

Surround yourself with good people.

Embrace perspective.

Choose to be better.

Happiness comes from the combination of all these things.

When you choose to look at things differently and share it with other people, you can be happy.

All of these things are in your control.

You can choose to surround yourself with good people. People that are helpful and influential to you. People that are genuinely good people that do the right thing, are kind, and are a joy to be around.

You can choose to embrace perspective. To look at things differently. To see things in a different light. To make negatives into positives. You do not have to follow the crowd.

You can choose to be better. When you don't like something, change it. You do not have to complain. You can spread good news instead of bad news. You can do what YOU want.

Don't think, oh great, that's a nice concept. It's also tactical. You can do these things right now. (Okay, finish reading the book first).

Make sure you know what is going on around you. Pay attention to things, learn about them, and make changes if needed.

Happiness is surrounding yourself with good people, embracing perspective, and choosing to be better.

This is the trifecta of life for many people, and we are happy.

Want to join us?

Chapter 6

The Attack

I thought I was having a heart attack.

Moments earlier, my Super Mario Brothers ring tone had gone off in the movie theater. I ALWAYS remembered to turn off my phone, but not this time. It's like Mario and Luigi were warning me of something.

We were watching our annual New Year's Eve movie (27 years and counting), when my heart began to race and I couldn't breathe. My blood pressure was going through the roof.

I went to the back of the theater to try and calm myself down.

Slowly, I began to relax and my heartbeat returned to almost normal.

Then, I was fine.

But I knew inside that I wasn't. Something was off.

A week later, it happened again.

Only this time, it went away much quicker.

And then the pain came.

It started in the middle of my stomach. A week later it went to the left. Another week went by and it went to the right. I thought I had a kuato in me. (Google that one!)

Then the worst part of all.

I couldn't eat.

I LOVE eating. And now I got some crazy thing going on and I can't eat. I would have half a sandwich and be stuffed...or the pain would start coming on. I lived off peanut butter sandwiches for 5 months.

I went to doctor after doctor after doctor. Nobody had a clue what was going on.

I heard celiac disease, hernia, crohn's, acid reflux...I think one dude even thought I was pregnant.

Months went by and still no answer. I started losing a lot of weight.

5 months later, I was down 40 pounds.

I never really saw myself as a big guy, but during this whole ordeal, I realized that something needed to change.

I had been around 215 pounds, eating junk, and not exercising. I couldn't allow myself to feel that way.

Finally after nearly 6 months, 7 doctors, and dozens of tests later, one of the docs said to me, "It could be your gall bladder."

So, they put me under, sliced and diced, and took out this little gall bladder the size of a golf ball (ironic, huh?).

It took about 2 years after that (with a little car accident mixed in) before I felt better again.

And it was a turning point in my life.

Not because of any kind of "close to death" thing. It wasn't that at all. It turned out to be minor. Anybody can have gall bladder attacks (but, man, I don't wish it on anyone).

It was a turning point because I had to look at my flaws.

I complained about things instead of changing them. I was 40 pounds overweight. I made excuses.

I wasn't as happy as I could be.

Then I read this:

[If you don't like something, change it. If you can't change it, change your attitude. Don't complain.]
-Maya Angelou

I made the conscious decision to not complain about things I can change. Instead, I needed to put forth the effort to make a difference.

It's not easy. And yes, sometimes I still catch myself complaining about the situation instead of helping it.

But just like practicing my golf game, or speaking, or writing…it becomes easier. And it becomes more ingrained.

Happy people don't complain. Happy people change.

Chapter 7

I Hope He's Nice

I'm not into celebrities all that much.

I think it's cool when I see someone on the street. I think it would be fun to golf with Justin Timberlake. And I'd like to have dinner with Natalie Portman.

But they are just people. And I hope they are nice.

Every sport has good players. And every sport has good people.

I'm more concerned with the good people.

I used to hear this from my mom every time we watched sports on TV. Kevin Garnett could be taking over a game, scoring from everywhere, and rebounding everything...and my mom would always say, "I hope he's nice."

Really, isn't that what it's all about?

You can never play at the highest level all the time. Because as you get older, as you play less, as you make time for other things, your skills will deteriorate.

So, focus on your character instead.

By putting more effort into character rather than skill, you'll be able to play good golf and have fun. And more importantly, sometimes you'll play crappy golf and still have fun.

And you can always be nice.

How people see you and what you really are.....are completely different. They see the outside stuff....what you have done, what you can do, what you look like.

But the inside stuff makes the difference.

You can always be nice.

In the fall of 2011, I sent out a letter to all the parents and students in my golf program. It was a simple letter with a strong message, basically saying that good people matter. And at the end of the day, the good people will outweigh good skill.

Here's the letter:

[I was a dorky kid.

I didn't really know it at the time....and by the time I figured it out, I really didn't care.

I was quiet. I played the saxophone (faked it my first two years!). I didn't like playing video games, but I could memorize the Legend of Zelda map and loved doing stats while my friends played old school (not old at the time) baseball. I had some close friends, but not a ton of them. I flew under the radar for most of my days in school.

When I got to high school, it was pretty much the same thing. Most people will say it's because my mom never gave me a chance to speak, because she did it so much (with gusts of up to 150 words per minute!) But, I knew a little better. I was just quiet.

I played golf, I reffed basketball and I didn't go out of Saturday nights because I wanted to watch Saturday Night Live. That was my fun.

And it was okay.

When I got to college, my freshman year roommate (who is now one of my great friends), talked less than I did. I realized that one of us had to talk, so it began... And now I speak for a living. Go figure.

From teaching for the past 13 years, I've run across a huge variety of kids. There are quiet kids and loud kids, athletes and non athletes, smart kids and happy kids and competitive kids. You name it, I've seen it.

The cool thing about all these kids is that it's all okay.

They are all kids who just want to be happy.

So no matter what kid comes through my camps, I try to make them happy.

It's kind of the same way I raise my kids. I get the question all the time....are they going to play golf? My response is always the same. "If they want to."

Because I don't care if my kids are good at golf or even play golf. I want them to be happy, kind kids. That's it. If Ethan wants to be a ballerina and Ella wants to be a ninja, that's cool with me. I just hope I have a happy ballerina and a kind ninja.

If you come to my golf camps, classes, events, or just see me at the range, I teach some pretty simple concepts. Be kind. Use your manners. Have fun. Do the right thing. The list goes on.

So as the first day, first week, and first month of school gets started, I want to address the kids in my classes, the kids who have taken them from me before, and the kids who will eventually take classes from me. What I teach during golf lessons is the same thing that will help you at school. I will welcome you with open arms when you take lessons from me. And, I'd rather have you be a great person than a great golfer.

Dear Students:

As you start this school year, I want you to remember a few things.

You are awesome. You are smart. You are fun.

You'll get nervous. You'll get tired. You'll do boring things in class. You'll do super fun things too. You'll meet new friends. You'll have teachers you like a lot and some you only like a little. You'll have easy work and tough work.

And it's all okay.

Lots of things happen at school. Some you'll like and some you won't. But through everything that happens...Be the nice kid.

When you see that kid in class that doesn't seem to have any friends...go talk with him. When you see that kid who dropped her books...go help her pick them up. When your teacher asks a question that you know...answer it. When your friends are doing something you know is wrong...walk away.

Be the nice kid.

I've taught golf to thousands of kids over the years and my goal is not to turn them into professional golfers. My goal is to help them become nice kids.

Go to school every day and see if you can make someone else in your class smile. Make someone else laugh. Make someone else feel good.

Be the nice kid.

It's easy to go along with the crowd and make fun of the kids who seem a little different. Guess what?..everyone is different. Everyone has their thing. Some kids are smarter than you, some kids have cooler clothes than you, some kids are better at sports than you. It doesn't matter...you have your thing too. Be the kid who can get along. The kid that is generous. The kid that is happy for other people. The kid that does the right thing. The kid that tries his best.

Be the nice kid.

If you have homework, do it. If you have a test, study for it. If you have a project, finish it.

Most of all, when your parents ask you to do something, listen to them. They aren't here to guide you in the wrong direction. They support you and love you. They are the ones that will help you the most along the way. Sure, there will be times when you think they are crazy and have no idea what they are talking about. Just trust them. They are here for YOU. Just like you treat your classmates at school, be nice to your parents.

Have fun at school, do what you're supposed to do, and be the nice kid.

I'll see you on the golf course soon.

Thanks,
Bryan]

The Good People of Golf

So, it got me thinking about surrounding myself with the good people of golf.

Who are the good people of golf? Who are the people that make your experience better? Who are the people that help you become happier?

1. The people you play with (friends and family)
2. Your teachers and coaches
3. The people who work at the facility you play

The cool thing is, besides family, you can choose every one of these people. You can choose to play at the happy course, with the happy people, and learn from the happy teachers. It's your choice.

The People you play with

These are the most important people that you will come across in your golf experience. Why? Because you have to hang out with these people for 4 hours! If they annoy you when you start, you're not going to have a very fun day, are you?

It really breaks down to two sorts of people. The people you choose to play with and the people that get matched up you. The first group is easy to get along with. They are your friends and your family. You've probably played golf with them before and you know the kind of people they are.

The uncomfortable group can be with players that get matched up with you. And I completely agree that this can be a touchy situation. You came out here to have fun (hopefully), and now you have to play with someone you don't know.

But it doesn't have to be that bad.

What if this person turns out to be your best friend? What if this person turns out to be your regular golfing buddy? What if this person teaches you something that you didn't know before?

Is that really that bad?

In my experience, if you're kind, friendly, and helpful, you'll never have a problem on the course. And later in your reading, you'll learn more about strengthening your relationships on and off the course.

Your teachers and coaches
Who got you into the game and who is continually helping you? This can play a crucial role in determining whether you love to play golf or want to give it up.

Most of it will depend on what YOU want to be taught. Are you out there to win every time you play (most happy golfers are not) or are you out there to have good experience? And what part of that experience is the most important to you?

A good teacher and coach will help you with the experience and show you how to get what you want out of the game.

Your teacher could be a parent, a friend, a co-worker, a spouse.

Watch out for the teachers that try to correct every little thing. And watch out for those that think the swing needs to be perfect.

The people who work at the facility you play
When you go to a course or driving range, how are you treated? And how to do you feel about that? Are they there just to take your money or will they actually talk to you like a real person?

Go find a place that you enjoy going to and have fun with the people working there.

To be happy in anything, you need support. The best support comes from the people who care about you and your experience. The best people are the ones who are generous enough to make sure that you have a good time and you are happy.

Who are the people that support you?

Who are the people that don't care what you have, but care who you are?

Who are your good people?

Chapter 8

The Bet

I grew up playing tennis, and basketball, and baseball. Golf didn't appear on the radar until around 8th grade.

Mostly because my dad only played a little and my mom and bro didn't play at all. We were exposed to other sports instead.

My parents had a timeshare that we went to every July and that's where I started to get the golf bug.

My dad would drive the golf cart and I would ride along with him. I never really played that much at first…just looked for golf balls in the woods. I still love looking for golf balls.

I played some more golf during the summer, but still tennis was on the top of the list.

In 9th grade, I played tennis on the real team, and golf on an intramural team.

In 10th grade, golf and tennis were both spring sports.

It was my first test at making an adult choice. My parents were cool with whatever I chose. But they told me that I had to choose.

I was pretty good at tennis. I knew I had a decent chance at making the Varsity team. I wasn't that good at golf yet, but I liked golf more.

So, I made my choice.

Golf.

Everybody told me I was nuts. Why did I choose something I liked over something I was better at?

Glad I didn't follow the crowd.

The first year on the team was fun. I learned how everything worked during practices and matches. We played every day, so my skill improved a little.

The season ended and it was time to play in the summer.

And that's when my dad made The Bet.

He told me that if I practiced 3 hours per week for the entire summer that he'd give me money. They had to be three separate days with at least an hour of practice each day.

I could do that. I loved golf, so this was going to be no problem.

So, I took the bet.

I probably should have figured out the terms of the bet before actually taking the bet because the payout wasn't great.

If I practiced 3 hours per week for 12 weeks in the summer, what would I get?

$10.

Yep, that's it. $10. Not $10 per day or per week. $10 total.

Now, I'm thinking, what the heck is the point of that. Why would I work that hard for a measly $10?

Then, the other Bryan kicked in. I wanted to prove him wrong. I wanted to make sure that he lost the bet. The $10 really doesn't matter, but seeing my dad (who wins every game he creates) lose...that's a great victory.

I practiced my butt off for the entire summer. I went to the Edinburgh putting green after dinner 3 nights a week to chip and putt. I tried out every chip in the book...high ones, low ones, spinning ones, top spin ones. I experimented with different ways of hitting shots. I goofed around. I played games with myself...and I had fun.

Now granted, some weeks were tough to get in my three hours of practice. I worked full time during the summer (at the jail in Plymouth before Parker's Lake Golf Center was there). And at night, sometimes I just wanted to sit down and watch TV. But in the back of my mind, I wanted to prove dad wrong.

In retrospect, I fell right into my dad's plan. He didn't care about the $10 either. And he knew that I would do what it took to make him lose the bet.

But...he didn't care about losing the bet. He just wanted me to get better at golf. He wanted me to learn work ethic. He wanted to be good at something...something I loved to do.

I didn't hit one single range ball that whole summer. My practice consisted of just chipping and putting. I'd play golf too, but that didn't count toward my practice time.

At the end of the summer, I had done it. I won $10 from my dad.

But it wasn't over yet.

That following spring when the high school season started again, I had moved up in the rotation. I had improved so much over the summer that I had gone from the #1 JV player (7th overall on the team) to the #1 Varsity player.

Thanks to dad.

He never pushed me. He just knew me. He supported me. He helped me with my choice.

Everything changed that summer. I found something that I enjoyed doing and my confidence grew.

I still couldn't talk to girls though.

So, what did I spend the $10 on?

Nothing.

It's still hanging on the wall in my childhood room at my dad's house. So every time I go over there, I am reminded of what he did for me.

Chapter 9

Jail Birdie

I used to visit my dad a lot at work.

It was fun.

I got to see his office, eat lunch with him, and say hi to his coworkers. He'd show me the ins and outs of running a business and all the cool things that they were going to do. It was all normal kid stuff.

Except my dad was the warden of a jail.

Now, the thing is, I really thought this was what all kids did. I was never scared or intimidated. I never felt out of place. I knew (and still do know) most of the people that worked there.

You'd think this goes against the standard of surrounding yourself with good people. But you'd be wrong. These inmates screwed up. They did something wrong. But the majority of them were decent people. Everyone makes mistakes. Their mistakes just called for harsher punishments.

My sophomore year in high school, I got a job at the jail. I mowed grass, weed whipped, painted…mostly general maintenance stuff.

On my first day, I ran over a paint can. And one time I put a stop sign on the wrong side of the post. It fit better.

Good thing I teach golf now.

When I worked for the jail, it was normal for us to go inside and eat everyday. The food was decent. Tuesday burger day was the best. The inmates ate in a cafeteria style gym, while the staff ate in their own separate dining room. This is where I got famous for making giant ice cream cookie sandwiches. Man, those were good.

Lunch could be adventurous sometimes though. If there was a call on the radio to break up a fight, everyone in the dining room would bolt out of there and go attend to the situation. And, they moved fast. I just sat there…ice cream sandwich in hand.

The jail is a working jail, which basically means that they try to put as many inmates as possible on various work crews. Some are janitors, some are cooks, some work in the laundry, and some work on what is now the driving range.

In 1996, they got an idea to build a driving range on the adjacent land, where a soy bean field once was. Conviction Creek Chip and Putt (Yep, it was intentionally named that) came a few years later and was built by inmates and employees at the jail.

When they first started building the range, I was a freshman in college, and I couldn't wait for it to open. They were going to transition some of the summer workers over to the range to work. It would be so much fun working on the range. I couldn't wait.

Then I got fired.

Let me clarify that…I didn't exactly get fired. I just didn't get asked back the following summer.

Why you may ask? Was it the stop sign incident? Nope. Too many ice cream sandwiches? Nope. It didn't really have a lot to do with me.

Long story short, my dad got accused of giving all the best jobs at the jail to his two sons.

I had worked there in the summer for 4 years, making a couple grand each summer. If making $2,000 during a three month summer is one of the best jobs out there, then everyone is in trouble.

It stemmed from an employee who had a beef with my dad. Instead of working it out with my dad, he went to the news. The local station picked up the story and did a 5 minute segment on nepotism (Don't worry, that's the biggest word I'll use in this book!)

The news story flashed my name and showed $55,000. They claimed I made $55,000 during my three months that summer. It was not even close to the truth, but it didn't really matter. The story wasn't necessarily stinging, but the publicity was out there. So, to cover itself, the county didn't rehire me or my brother.

The following summer, I got lucky. The local Park and Rec department ran a couple golf programs for kids and adults, and the instructor was leaving. Since, I played golf in high school and was playing in college at the time, I figured I'd have a decent chance at it.

So, I applied...and got it.

At the same time, the city was looking to move their golf programs to another facility. Oh, and what facility just happened to be opening that same summer?...Parker's Lake Golf Center, right next to the jail. So, that's been my home for the last 13 years.

I built the City of Plymouth programs from 6 classes to about 40 in a few years. Enrollment jumped and I started on my career path (even though as a 19 year old college kid, I really didn't know it at the time).

A few years later, I turned pro and opened the Bryan Skavnak Golf Academy.

That day I didn't get rehired was a good day. Even though, at the time, it may have been change I didn't want.

But change is inevitable.

Change is just an opportunity. An opportunity to do something different. And opportunity to make yourself better.

It's your choice what you'll do with the change.

Chapter 10

9 Traits of Happy Golfers

I was a slammer.

I wasn't a thrower. I wasn't a swearer. (Is that a word?) My thing was slamming.

And I am not proud of it.

When I was younger, I took golf a little too seriously.

I didn't enjoy the people I was playing with. I only cared about my score. I had to hit every shot perfectly.

And if it wasn't perfect, I'd slam my club.

Usually, it was a quick slam and I was done with it. But, sometimes, I'd have trouble letting go of my anger.

That did nothing but compound the problem.

I'd hit more bad shots, more slams, more bad shots, more slams....and pretty soon, I didn't even want to be out there any more.

I was having no fun at all. And, I was no fun to play with.

That was not the person I wanted to be.
Why would I want to spend 4 hours of my day being miserable?
Why would I want to isolate my friends and family?
Why was I acting like a jerk over a game?
Why did the score really matter that much?

Why wasn't I happy? Why wasn't I having fun?

Looking back, it usually resulted from:

1. Focusing too much on the score
2. Thinking I should be playing better, even though I wasn't putting in the practice time.
3. Thinking about other things when I was playing.
4. Not having any fun with my playing partners, but not spending the effort to get to know them.
5. Blaming the weather or the course or some other distraction for my bad play.

And I started to think about happiness more...

Swimming gets it

Think of swimming....when you say to your friends, "Hey want to go swimming?", do they say, "Okay, cool, I'll bring my goggles, my cap, and the ropes. You bring the starting block, and the clock, so we can time each other."

Heck, no.

Let's go swim means, let's go splash around in the water, play a few games, dunk each other, and have some fun.

Nobody thinks that "Let's go swim" means "Let's go race."

That's a big problem with golf.

Most people think "Let's go golf" means "Let's go play 9 or 18 holes, keep score, and then compare how we played at the end."

To me, "Let's go golf" means hitting some good shots and some not so good shots, finding some golf balls, having a good walk, and getting some food.

To other people, "Let's go golf" means being outside. It means going to the driving range. It means playing mini putt with the kids. It means playing 3 holes and then eating a good dinner.

Fred gets it

When I first started teaching golf, I was determined to be different. And, I had one simple goal: To provide happiness.

Then something cool happened.

I was introduced to this book called Extraordinary Golf by Fred Shoemaker. Here's an excerpt from this awesome book:

["If an average golfer takes 90 shots in a round, and each shot takes about two seconds, that adds up to only about three minutes of actual play. The pre-shot routine takes anywhere from 5 to 10 seconds, which adds another ten seconds or so. That leaves more than three hours and forty-five minutes of time between shots in a typical four hour round - about 95 percent of the round. This is time where you are simply out on the course, walking (or riding) to your next shot.

The traditional method of teaching golf focuses almost exclusively on the 5 percent of swing time and ignores the other 95 percent of the round. I've come to realize that the people that are most likely to improve beyond what is ordinary are people who have mastered the time between shots. I'm not talking about strategy or positive thinking or simply "doing things differently". I'm talking about a new way to "be" out on the course. I'm talking about being a golfer. The best and most lasting changes take place when a person is essentially "being different"."]

I love "being different."

Can you imagine how much more fun golf could be if you thought about it differently? If you didn't concern yourself with what is typical "golf."

My mom's card club gets it

I remember when my mom had her card club over to play.

They always played 500 and they were always super loud. Not loud in a bad way. They were laughing, joking, telling stories....oh, and playing a little cards.

But they didn't really care about the cards. Sure, there were a few competitive ones in the bunch and yes, they tried their best. But it wasn't about who had the most points at the end.

It was getting together a bunch of friends once a month to have some fun.

There were 8 of them in the group (always rotating because someone could never make it). They had a big spread of food on the table and snacks on the cards tables.

I would always come downstairs and pretend like I had to ask my mom a question....then she'd let me eat some food... and maybe have a piece of famous ice cream pie.

Golf should be the same way. A bunch of friends getting together, laughing and having fun....and playing a little golf.

Golf is the excuse to get together. Cards were my mom's excuse.

My golf classes get it

I don't condone drinking and driving.

Although I usually do it a few times a year.

On purpose.

With about 8 other people.

I know. I know. What's the catch?

Here it is:

I teaching a driving class (How to hit your driver better) and I bring beer.

What was that? Yeah. Best class ever.

Now here's the weird thing. I have never had a beer on the golf course.

Never.

I like golf so much that when I get a chance to play, I just play.

I can have something after.

But for this class, I bring beer for the students and we hit our driver.

I do this for a few reasons.

1. It helps some people relax.
2. It magically turns it into a social event rather than a golf lesson.

When that first bottle is popped, everyone seems to let out a collective sigh. It turns from learning this game to being with friends, talking, and, oh yeah, playing a little golf.

My kids get it

I love taking my kids to watch the Twins play at Target Field. They last about 6 innings right now (which ironically is about how long the Twins lasted this season), and I'm completely cool with it.

My kids also have no idea what's going on down on the field.

Sure, they know a couple players....Joe Mauer, Nishioka (only because Ethan has shoes of the same name). But they don't understand how to play the game yet.

What they do understand is the experience.

They understand that when we go to Target Field, we get to wear our Twins T-shirt. We get to eat peanuts (I swear my kids are elephants with all the peanuts they eat). We get to listen to music played on the intercom. We get to play games in between innings. My kids like the "everything else" involved with the game.

Golf is about the "everything else" too.

Happiness is in the "everything else."

Happy Golfers get it

I played golf in high school, in college, and in tournaments after college. I have taught over 10,000 people in my career. I've studied the people who "get it" and the people who constantly make golf into a personal demon.

I can relate. I was one of those people that took a long time to understand that the golf part really isn't the important part.

When I was growing up, there wasn't a handbook or a teacher that taught the "everything else" of golf. I wasn't planning on going to the PGA Tour, but every teacher seemed to be trying to teach swing and not experience. I wanted to learn the basics and learn to have more fun playing the game. I wanted to learn how to be happy playing golf.

Since there wasn't a handbook on how to be happy on the course, I decided to start documenting it myself.

I finally wanted to break down the people that had the best time on the course. The people that you LOVED to play with. These people are not just happy on the course, but in other areas of their life too.

They are young, old, beginner, and experienced. They may play a couple times a year or many times per week.

So after studying people, and playing, and seeing what kind of results that people can actually get from being around the game, I put together the:

9 Traits of Happy Golfers

1. Happy Golfers don't care about their score.

They may play a round and then completely forget about what they just shot. Many of the happiest golfers don't even keep score. They go out, hit some shots, and have a good time with their friends. They may keep score in alternate ways like using match play scoring or playing different games on every hole.

2. Happy Golfers make the game social.

Happy Golfers care who they play with....they invite friends and family that they know they'll have fun with. It's tough for a happy golfer when the get matched up with another twosome. But happy golfers make it social nonetheless. They engage the people they are playing with and enjoy the time spent with PEOPLE.

3. Happy Golfers extend their time on the course.

What does this exactly mean? Happy golfers make sure that when the round is done, they stick around at the clubhouse and have dinner. Or they go out for ice cream with the kids. Or they hit up my personal fave...Buffalo Wild Wings. Just because the game is done, doesn't mean the experience is done.

4. Happy Golfers don't play by the rules.

I know this one sounds strange. There are a ton of rules of golf that are simply confusing. Many golfers don't know these rules and do not intentionally break them. They do what seems fair. And that's the takeaway for happy golfers....<u>if you're not sure of what to do, do what seems fair.</u>

5. Happy Golfers understand that not every shot will be perfect.

You probably only hit one or two shots that feel exactly the way you thought it would. The ball that flies great in the air, and lands exactly where you thought. Otherwise, everything else is just a miss. Sometimes they are really good misses, sometimes they are really bad misses.
A happy golfer understands the difference.

6. Happy Golfers accept responsibility and move on.

When a not-so-good shot appears, a happy golfer is able to forget about it quickly and move on to the next one. Because, they know that if they hold on, it only results in more not-so-good ones.

7. Happy Golfers make decisions and play fast.

Happy golfers don't think about every shot. They already have a plan in mind and they try and execute the plan. They move along and do what they are supposed to do, always trying to make good decisions. If they are ready, they go for it.

8. Happy Golfers are aware of everything else around them.

Happy golfers can hear the birds chirp. They can hear the train whistle. They feel the warmth of the sunshine. They see and hear everything and don't let anything distract them from their enjoyment of the game. You'll never hear an excuse from a happy golfer that "The lawnmower distracted me" or "The beverage cart got in my way." Happy golfers like beverage cart girls. I married one.

9. Happy Golfers remember good shots, not bad ones.

When you get to a hole, there is always that memory of something. Remember that time I got a hole in one here. Remember that time that lawnmower ran over my ball. Most people tend to focus on the negative in this situation. Remember that time I went in the water. Remember last time when I got a 10. Happy Golfers can approach a hole and remember the positives and compound those positives.

This is what I have found in many of the happiest people that play. They are lessons that can easily be slid into other areas of life too. (Replace "Golfers" with "People" and you'll see what I mean).

They are not just concepts, but tactics. They are things that you can do right now to be a happier golfer and a happier person. Things that make your experience better.

Because ultimately, it's the experience that's important.

And it's the experience that makes you happy.

Chapter 11

The Secret to Playing Happy Golf

It's the happy experience we're after, right?

So, why do so many people come to me and other golf pros trying to fix something?

I want to fix this. I'm doing this. I can't get rid of this.

I 100% agree that if you're better at something, you usually have more fun with it.

But, I also believe that if you have fun with something, there is a better chance you'll learn it more quickly.

So that's why I approach it differently. That's why the fun comes first. The experience comes first.

The perfection of your swing doesn't matter, because you're not trying to build a swing. You're trying to play a game.

Remember this from last chapter....

["If an average golfer takes 90 shots in a round, and each shot takes about two seconds, that adds up to only about three minutes of actual play. The pre-shot routine takes anywhere from 5 to 10 seconds, which adds another ten seconds or so. That leaves more than three hours and forty-five minutes of time between shots in a typical four hour round - about 95 percent of the round. This is time where you are simply out on the course, walking (or riding) to your next shot."]

If you hammer out the math, it's about 15 minutes of actual time hitting the ball.

Wouldn't you think the rest of the time playing has a greater impact on your enjoyment than those 15 minutes of ball hitting?

What if you had more fun first, got what you wanted out of the game, and let the score handle itself?

Yet, people only work on the swing and score part of the experience.

This is one major thing that non-golfers (and most golfers) don't understand. You can have a great time with golf and not be good at it. It's not about how well you hit a little white ball.

There are myths about golf that are really just that...myths. Just like there are myths about unicorns, and giants, and Nickelback being good. People heard it from someone who heard it from someone. It travels around and now everyone starts believing it.

Golf Myth #1
Golf is hard

Golf is as hard as you make it. To some people math is hard. To some people skateboarding is hard. Think of it this way. It's hard to do what? What is the goal? If you're goal is to hit it 500 yards, then yes, golf is hard. If your goal is to enjoy the time with your friends on the course, then no way that golf should be hard.

Golf Myth #2
Golf takes too long

If you were on tv playing for a million bucks every week, golf gets a little tedious. It can take a while. 18 holes of golf can take 4-5 hours. 9 holes can take around 2. But what if you just want to take your kids out to hit a bucket of balls at the range? You can do that as slowly or as quickly as you'd like. What if you just want to go out and putt around for a few minutes?

Golf Myth #3
Golf is boring

Can't anything and everything be boring? Again, if you want to have fun with it, have fun with it. Find ways to make it less boring. Play games, talk with other people, ride on a cart, and look for golf balls. Find what part of the experience makes you excited and keep at it.

Golf Myth #4
My swing needs to be perfect

That's just dumb. Nothing has to be perfect. Oh yeah, and nothing CAN be perfect. There are always different things that are going on; different stance, different lie, different grass, different wind. The only thing you have to do is make the ball go toward where you want it to go. Is it going to go there every time? No way. Otherwise you'd be on TV. Play a game. Don't play a swing.

So, get rid of the myths and get selfish for a moment.

What do YOU want?

The first thing you need to decide to have a truly happy golf experience is why you are out there.

I am playing golf today, so that I can _____.

Nobody says, "I am playing golf today, so that I can get really mad, slam my clubs, lose money to my buddies, and then go home and argue with my wife about why I was gone so long."

It's your choice. What do you want to get out of the day?

Ask yourself some questions. Why am I playing this game? What do I want to get out of it? What are the important things for me?

Focus on the other part of golf. The "everything else."

How would your experience change?

What you are going to do for the other 3 hours and 45 minutes when you're not hitting the ball?

Focus on the experience.

Your experience playing the game is different than anyone else. What you want from golf is different than what someone else wants.

These are the essential parts of your golf experience.

1. Who you play with? (Friends, Family, Co-workers, strangers)
2. Where you play? (Facility)
3. Why you play? (Your decision - The reason you are there)
4. What format you play? (Tournament, with friends, etc)
5. How you play? (Your skill level)

It's not all about hitting every shot perfect. It might not even be about hitting any shots perfect...or far, or straight.

Are you going to have meaningful conversations with your group? Are you going to relax and enjoy nature? Are you going to strike up a business deal? Are you going to have a great time with your family?

And, if you want to have a much better experience…

Don't keep score.

I was a decent high school player. I played #1 Varsity on a bad team. Never broke 80 in high school. Never went to state. College was better. I played a few tournaments my freshman and sophomore years. Finished 10th in a tournament. Then some better players came along and they played instead.

But, I got really good at golf after college. I realized that I didn't have to be scared anymore. Cause I was scared. I didn't want to hit a bad shot in front of people (There's that fear thing again!). I felt like my score was the only thing that mattered.

After college, I took my playing test, passed on the first time, and turned pro. Then I fell into what many pros realize. I'm around golf all day long, teaching it, watching it, but I don't get to play.

So when I did play, I really just played. I didn't care what number I got on a hole. I just hit a shot and moved on. I got to play with my dad and my friends and that's what was really important.

Over the next few years, I realized that score didn't matter at all. My golf score did not determine the kind of person that I was.

So, I stopped keeping score.

I'd only keep score in tournaments, and I didn't play that many tournaments anyway, so it didn't matter. I just started hitting shots.

I didn't worry about making pars and birdies. I just went up, hit a shot, and continued on my way. I didn't think about it. I didn't care about where my ball went. Sure, I was making my ball go toward a target, but I didn't beat myself up if I didn't hit the target.

If someone asked to write down my score at the end of the hole, I'd simply say, "I don't keep score."

I got some weird looks and questions right away, but I had been playing golf for a long time. I wanted to do something different (and it's okay to be different!).

I loved it because now I was playing for the reasons I wanted to play.

I was spending time with people who were important to me. I was able to be creative with my shots. And I had some great stories from my rounds.

I still do not keep score. Yes, I have an idea of where I'm at during the round, but it doesn't concern me.

For some people, the score is all that's important. And it's the fear of not living up to a good score that prevents people from enjoying the day.

It's kind of crazy how a number can affect us.

People come to me wanting to break 100 or break 90 or 80 or whatever. The fixation with this number drives people to think they are inadequate or lacking in skill.

Totally false.

Never judge your character by the score you shoot.

It's just a number.

A few years ago I helped out at another golf course on the weekends. A co-worker of mine asked if I wanted to play after we were done with our shift. I wanted to get home, shower up, and go out with my girlfriend. I know what you're thinking..."he didn't want to golf?" Scratch that, you were probably thinking, "He had a girlfriend?!"

Reluctantly, I told him that I'd play 9 holes with him.

I had to open the course that day (get there at 5:30 in the morning and explain to the players that, "No, sir, you're not allowed to play the course when it's dark outside still." Or, "Seriously, you want a hot dog? It's 7:15am."

So, needless to say, I was a little on the sleepy side when I started playing that afternoon.

We got matched up with a couple of our regulars and played the back nine first. I had a great time laughing and talking with the guys, but my mind was on getting home after 9 holes.

I had all pars up until the 15 hole. I birdied 16, parred 17, and birdied 18. So after 9 holes, I was 2 under. (You're right, I preach about not keeping score. And I didn't. But after playing as long as I have, you have an idea where you're at.)

I had a fun time, but still wanted to get home.

I must have been half asleep because my co-worker convinced me to play another 9 holes.

I'm still not sure why I played.

I birdied number 1.

I birdied number 2.

I parred number 3.

I birdied number 4.

I was now 5 under after 13 holes. The course record at the time was 5 under.

And then I shocked everyone in the group.

"I'm going home."

"What?!" That was the consensus in the group. They didn't know what to say. They all tried to convince me stay, but I wanted to go home.

I wanted to eat some food, I wanted to get home at a reasonable time, and I wanted to see my not fake girlfriend.

The number didn't matter to me. Playing the game for the score is not the reason I play. I play to be with friends. I play to hit crazy shots. I play to tell stories.

So, I told them, "I'm playing this hole and it's my last one."

I birdied that one too.

Then walked to my car.

The secret to golf is easy.

Stop keeping score.

The score does not matter. The score does not determine your character.

I hear people all the time say, "I suck" or "I'm terrible" or "I'm so bad."

Wrong.

It's not you that sucks or is terrible or is so bad. It's your score.

There have been times when I feel like I've played great and have had a higher score. There have times that I played crappy and scored okay.

The score should not determine your happiness.

I used to work at another golf course where I manned the front desk.

Every person that walked in was treated the same. And, the more I got to know them, the more I teased them. It was just a way to break the ice and be more personable with them.

Everyone got a greeting and most people's response to the greeting was pretty similar.
"How's it going?" Good.
"How are you doing today?" Pretty good.
"How have you been?" I've been good.

I don't mind good.

It's a standard answer. Mostly because the person doesn't want to say too much and I think it's how we are wired to respond.

But one morning, I got a stupid answer.

A guy came in to check in for his tee time. I asked him, "How are you doing today?"

His answer:

"I'm not sure. I'll tell you after I play."

What?!

He's going to let his golf game determine his mood for the day?

So if he plays bad, he'll be mad and if he plays good, he'll be happy?

Here's the thing....usually people who let other things determine their happiness are never truly happy anyway. They will always find a fault in something. They will always blame and always think negatively. There is never a "good enough."

Play your game with the idea of having a good experience. Realize that of the list of things you want to enjoy on the course, score is way near the bottom.

In golf lessons, I talk a lot about focusing on the target, rather than on the ball. Don't try to hit the ball. Try to make the ball go toward a target.

When you play catch, you are trying to throw the ball to a person. You're not just chucking it up in the air in hopes it goes to the target.

Most people work on their swing in hopes that swing will eventually be good enough to make the ball go where they want it to go.

What if you focused on the target and your swing adjusted for that target?

What if you focused on the experience you want and let the rest fall into place?

Instead of constant planning, tweaking, and fixing, why not focus on what outcome you want and adjust your plans from there?

Think the same way when you are going to play the game. Your target may be to learn more about your playing partners. Your target may be to enjoy being outside for the day. Your target may be watching your kids smile.

Whatever your target may be, do things that get closer to that target.

If you want to know your playing partners better, ask more questions. Share more information.

If you want to enjoy nature, then keep your head up when you're walking. Listen better. Look around more.

If you want to see your kids smile more, give them encouragement. Smile more yourself. Be an example.

If you want to be happier, why not find out what will make you happier first, instead of doing a bunch of things in hope that it will make you happier?

My target is no longer the score because I don't want a score to determine who I am and the experience I have.

I challenge you to not let your happiness be determined by what you do, or what you have, but by who you are.

When Darren Clarke won the British Open earlier in 2011, his coach gave him one simple goal,

"Let your attitude determine your game, don't let your game determine your attitude."

Do that and I promise you that you'll be happier.

Chapter 12

The Fortunate 5

We used to joke that my mom should run for mayor of her city.

Not because she knew anything about politics or wanted to be in the public eye, but because she knew everyone.

She had this ability to talk to her friends on the phone for hours, go play cards and talk some more, then come home and talk with us.

She's still the only person I know who could strike up a conversation with a stranger in the grocery store, and figure out that she knew this person's uncle's landlord's brother's cousin's groomsman.

At her funeral, people showed up from all over. They traveled from different cities, they took off work, and they showed support. Mostly because it's the same thing she would have done. (Except for the work part...she "retired" when I was born)

The church told us it was the biggest funeral they ever had. People were spilling out of the gathering space and there were enough bars and desserts (mom's favorite) for entire cities.

She was a star at forming relationships; relationships that really mattered. Where you could talk to people about anything and have a genuine connection.

How was this possible? How did my mom have so many friends, so many acquaintances, and so many people who wanted to be around her?

She didn't have a game plan. It was her personality to be kind and generous. She interacted in a way that always showed a smile.

Because I was the quiet kid, I wasn't good at forming bonds like she was. Really nobody was.

But I watched to see what she did.

I wanted to know what she did differently to attract such a wide array of good people. Below are the 5 things that she would do. If you want to attract good people to you, take these to heart. These are the Fortunate 5.

Give - Give of your time. Give help. Give attention. Give a compliment. Give advice. Give a gift. Give affection. Give something that the other person needs to feel happier. Simple as that. Give what you have to other people. This is the first key to any relationship. Even if you don't do anything else on this list, do this one. Give.

Ask - Ask questions. But ask personal questions. Ask about the other person's interests. Ask about feelings, and highs and lows. Ask about dreams and hopes. Ask things that others wouldn't.

Listen - Really listen. Be there to listen whenever it's needed. Listen for details or hints or small things. The more you listen, the more you're able to ask.

Laugh - Find the humor in every situation. Smile and laugh...but really mean it.

Play - Make things social. Go out for breakfast or lunch. Join leagues. Take up new things. Go to events. Play cards. Play games. Have an avenue to constantly get together...card club, church group, school group.

Golf is a perfect avenue for forming real, meaningful relationships. You are able to give time to another person, ask questions, listen intently, and laugh at bad shots...all while playing a game.

Just by trying to form real relationships, you will see your experience elevated. You will have more fun. And you won't worry about the golf because you'll be too busy making friends.

Chapter 13

Let's Get Ready to Scrumble

I have golf values.

So do you. Even if you don't play golf.

Because these golf values are identical to your core values and what makes you who you are. These are the things that you feel are important.

My golf values are good people, good course, good meal, and good attitude.

If I have all 4 of these things, I have an awesome time. Even if I only have three of them, I usually have a great time too.

So a few years back (11 to be exact), my dad and I wanted to start a tournament for our friends that combined all of our golf values.

Thus was born THE SCRUMBLE.

The Scrumble is always played on the first day of the Minnesota State Fair. It's a partner event where we play best ball on the par 4s, alternate shot on the par 5s, and both balls on the par 3s.

We fill up every year and have a waiting list.

The Scrumble is basically a collection of some good, but mostly mediocre golfers, having a good time, making fun of each other, playing for prizes that we stagger.

And The Scrumble operates under a few select principles (this is taken directly from our Scrumble handout):

[First, prizes are staggered meaning that good prizes and not so good prizes are mixed throughout the placement results. You may receive a "better" prize finishing farther down the list and that reinforces our motto that "you don't have to be a good golfer to win a good prize". The field is split into two (2) Divisions. The first 16 teams make-up the Upper Division and the remaining 16 teams make-up the Lower Division.

The Second Principle centers on our 100% guarantee. No matter if your prize is the wrong size, wrong color or wrong fit or if you have 3 more like it at home, be advised of our prize principle - - We don't care! We are 100% satisfied with the prizes even if you are not. Feel free to trade prizes if you can or leave them in front of someone else's chair and slowly sneak away.

The Third Principle focuses on Second Place in each Division. We choose not to reward second and eighteenth place and consider these teams to be the first losers. Therefore, we feel that the biggest losers shouldn't be rewarded and therefore they receive nothing. Fate seems to agree, and the appropriate teams seem to fall-in to these positions.

The Fourth Principle is being honorable in your performance. This includes the sharing of any cash winnings with your partner, being generous to service staff, and leaving the facilities in good shape.]

This encourages people just to play and have fun.

We give away a trophy that we found in a dumpster. And a giant check like Happy Gilmore would cash.

We have a raffle, a huge turkey dinner, and a ton of laughs.

The Scrumble is just the way we try to put some fun into golf by gathering up the good people we know and spending time with them.

So, why do we call it The Scrumble?

Again...taken from our Scrumble handout:

[Back in the early 1970's, an amateur playing in the Bob Hope Desert Classic Pro-am event made history.

The story goes that this person, playing in a Pro-am Scramble prior to the PGA tournament, got involved in a serious conflict with his playing partners and the group's assigned Pro. It seems that this person, Louis B. Gruemfodder, got so competitive, nasty, belligerent, arrogant, etc. that his own team attempted to remove him from play. It got physical, the Pro got punched and Louis got banned from future PGA sponsored events forever.

Local news referred to the incident as the Scramble that turned into a Rumble. We have simply joined the two words to form "The Scrumble" and designed a format that relies on teamwork and the competitive individualism of a Louis Gruemfodder. The 1st Place Trophy and a "Big Check" is awarded in his name.

As always in "The Scrumble", the taunting light remains on and you need to prepare yourself for the taunts, trials, and tribulations that this event may offer.]

The best part about this Gruemfodder story is that it's completely made up. My dad and I wanted a back story to the name, and thought of this in a hot tub. Until now, nobody knew it was made up.

Go determine your golf values.

What is important to you? Why do you want to play? What do you want from the game? What will make you happy?

We use The Scrumble as our gathering of good people because it's what we value.

If you could create a great experience based on your values, what would it look like?

Got it in your mind? Good.

Now, go do it.

Chapter 14

Golf's Characters

I go to the State Fair for the same two reasons everybody else does.

To visit the 4-H barn and to swear at carnies.

Oh, wait, wrong book.

I go to eat and to people watch.

There is nothing better than getting a dairy barn malt, sitting on the curb, and watching the freaks go by.

On the flip side, I'm sure that there is someone sitting on an opposite curb somewhere watching that weirdo in the golf flip flops eat his malt.

It's okay, we're all weird.

Every school, every company, every team, every person everywhere has their quirks. And it's these quirks that can make things fun.

Can you imagine if the whole world was made up of people who thought like you, acted like you, and talked like you?

Holy cow, I'd have a Bryan war.

The golf course is no exception to the quirkiness. In fact, I would argue that golf has some of the goofiest characters.

The League

My dad plays in his work golf league every Tuesday. A few guys will go out around 1pm to play 9 holes and then the rest of the league will join in around 3:30.

In high school, on Tuesdays (when we didn't have golf practice), I signed myself out (always told them I had to see my parole officer. Remember my dad worked at a jail) to go play golf with those goofballs. Granted, my parents were fine with it. Obviously my dad knew that I was skipping school, since I played golf with him. I got good grades, I did my homework. It wasn't a problem.

This league is awesome.

This is the state fair of golf leagues.

There is the guy who has the greatest southern drawl you've ever heard. The guy called Kool Aid. The Evil Doer. The guy who grunts like an elephant.

This is the only league whose members get lost on the course.

We've played golf with this group for years and years. And throughout those years, we've played in some fun tournaments together. And they produced even more characters.

There was the guy who walked right through a screen door to get more food. There was the guy who snapped two clubs over his leg in the same round. There was the guy who could string together so many swear words that George Carlin would be embarrassed. There was the guy with giant hands, the guy with giant feet (oh wait, that was me), and the guy with the giant nose. There was the fast guy and the slow guy. And Rollie, the guy with one leg...

During one Irish Open (another of our fun tournaments), we got held up on the 3rd hole. We just stopped. We couldn't figure out why. Quickly word got out....Rollie broke his leg. Holy cow! Rollie broke his leg?! We were playing golf and he broke his leg?! About 20 minutes later, we started moving again...after Rollie went back to his house and got a new leg. Yeah, Rollie broke his wooden leg.

Mr. Foosball

I played golf one day with a friend and we got matched up with another guy.

Walking down the first fairway, we started talking and I asked him what he did for a living.

"I play foosball."

I did a double take and then asked to clarify (not in a bad way).

"You play foosball?"

"Yep."

Now, I was really interested in how someone can play foosball for a living.

Me: "How does that work?"

Mr. Foosball: "I go around to different bars and play people. I enter tournaments and travel around."

Me: "Can you support yourself doing that?"

Mr. Foosball: If I play well enough. I took home about 10 grand last year.

After talking with Mr. Foosball the entire round, I learned more about the game and the strategy than I could have imagined. Not unlike golf, it was a lot of offense and defense. Finding out the information and then making your choice.

I still have no idea how he could live off 10 grand a year, so he either didn't tell me what he really did, or the guy was frugal. Either way, it didn't matter to me. I talked to an interesting guy for 4 hours and learned about a game that I really had no previous interest in.

The experience was awesome.

On the flip side, I've played golf with some real jerks too. And when I was younger, I probably was the jerk more than I'd like to admit. These people take the game more seriously than the interaction. They see the score as important and the people as secondary.

I encourage you to look at your quirks and your strange traits. The things you know that others might find interesting. The places you've been, the things you've learned, the fun things you've done...these are all important to the people around you.

Sure, I'm telling you a little of my story throughout this book, but your story is important too. Probably more important.

Everyone can bring something to the course (or wherever you are) to engage, entertain, and help other people.

Your inner weirdness is the key to this. Don't be afraid of your story. Let other people know about it and let them determine what they like about it.

Everyone has a quirk. Everyone has that thing where you say, "Really, that's kind of weird."

But it doesn't matter.

The quirks make it fun. And if you're a good person, you're a good person. Even if you're a goofball, even if people don't understand you, even if you do some strange things, you can still be a good person.

I'll be nice to you. You be nice to me.

I don't care if you have 40 beers on the course, or embarrass yourself flirting with the beverage cart girl. It doesn't matter if you watch the golf channel 24/7 or have no clue how to play.

Just be a good person and don't be afraid of your story. Your relationships and happiness will grow.

And if you're good at foosball, I want to know. But if you like Nickelback, stay away from me.

Remember that golf is about the people. It's about the memories you share. It's about the time you spend together. You'll swing the club countless times in your life, but there may be only one time you see a grown man walk through a screen door to get that last cookie.

Chapter 15

The Day I Turned Pro

It was one simple question.

What's the worst that can happen?

In order to turn pro and go down the path of a PGA Golf Professional, you first have to take a playing test.

I was nervous about it. I had played golf for a while, and the score I needed to pass, I had shot before. But, the situation was different. It was a career defining round.

If I passed, I got into the PGA program and would start working my way down the golf pro path. If I didn't pass, I was going to be the joke of all my friends, family, and students. Okay, that probably wasn't going to happen, but that's what it felt like.

On the day before the test, I was standing on the driving range observing a lesson given by another instructor, and the student asked about the playing test. I explained to him how it worked.

He asked a few more questions and then said, "So, if you don't pass, what's the worst that can happen?"

I thought about it for a second and came up with the most logical answer I could.

"I just take it again."

Nobody was going to explode. Golf wasn't going to be cancelled. People weren't going to hate me.

I just would have to take it again.

So, that's the attitude I took going into the round.

This is how the playing test works.

I had to shoot 15 shots over the course rating for 36 holes. I know. That's sounds like gibberish. Without going into too many details, my score had to be 156 or better for 36 holes.

I decided later in the summer to turn pro, and all the Minnesota testing locations were full, so I traveled to Onalaska, Wisconsin. I didn't even know that was a place.

I grabbed my college roomie as my caddy and we headed out to the course.

I woke up the next morning ready to play. I wasn't nervous. I was actually excited.

I started bogey, bogey, bogey, bogey.

Crap.

That was not the start I expected.

We were standing on the 5th tee box and a set of words came from my roomie's mouth that I'll never forget.

"Skavnak, quit f**king around."

Another simple statement. Maybe a little stronger than "What's the worst that can happen?"

If you knew him, he's the nicest guy in the world, just doesn't exactly have a Mr. Rogers mouth.

So I don't bore you with shot by shot analysis, I was 4 over the first 4 holes and I was 6 over the next 31 holes.

I approached the last hole of the day. It was a 390 yard, par 4, with water and sand all around it.

I was 4 shots inside the number I needed to pass. I thought to myself that I could make an 8 and still pass.

Bad thought.

I got ahead of myself.

I decided to play it safe and hit a 2 iron off the tee. I barely hit the top part of the ball and it sailed low to the ground and rolled out about 220 yards. I got lucky.

I walked up to my second shot and realized I was in a pretty good spot. I had 170 yards left. Easy little 6 iron.

The problem was that the shot was 170 yards over water, over sand, to an elevated green. I would have to hit a near perfect shot to get it on the green.

But I had 4 shots to play with.

So I did what any person in my situation would do.

I got up to the ball, picked my target, and hit my shot.

My ball landed 90 yards short of the green.

I had done it on purpose.

See, I had to make a choice.

Do I try to pull off the 170 yard shot over water and over sand (that I knew I could do and had done many times before)? Or, do I use strategy, turn 90 degrees sideways, and hit a little bump away from the water and sand to put myself in a better position?

Which one was going to be the right choice?

I didn't know. But I had to make the choice.

In golf, there is a lot of talk about staying committed to the shot. Golfers who are not committed tend to have more bad shots and frustration than those who do.

The first thing you have to do to stay committed is make a choice. Decide what you are going to do. The choice makes things clearer. The choice limits other distractions.

I walked to my ball, grabbed my sand wedge and stuck that 90 yard shot about 15 feet away.

When I got to the green, I lagged a putt, knocked in my bogey 5, and moved a step closer to becoming a PGA pro.

Happiness doesn't result from the correct choice. It results from making any choice. Because sometimes you choose right and sometimes you choose wrong. But you learn from those choices.

Be proud of yourself that you made a choice at all because many people are too scared to choose and go through life dreading decisions. Choose to be better.

Chapter 16

How Dancing in Public Crushed My Fear

I experimented in college.

There were drugs, alcohol, parties, and access to almost anything. Kids were constantly being pressured to do things that they hadn't done before.

And I fell into the trap.

Although... I didn't do the drugs, and I didn't drink (until I was 21. Seriously. Nobody believes me. But I had more important things to do).

No, my peer pressure was much worse. And I'm not proud of it.

I listened to country music.

Even saying it now makes me want to throw up on my keyboard.

For one solid month during my freshman year of college, I listened to country music. My roommate liked it, there was this girl, and Tupac just "died." Come on, I was going through some stuff.

Don't worry, we all make mistakes. Plus, my kids aren't named Toby or Keith, so we're cool.

Music has been a part of my life since I was a little kid. I come from a very musical family.

And, by musical, I mean that my brother played in a few college bands; my mom constantly sang the wrong lyrics to every song imaginable when we were growing up; I faked my way through the saxophone in grade school; and my dad just recently learned how to use his ipod.

So yeah, we're musical in the sense that we LIKE music. We don't have a lot of talent surrounding music. We just really enjoy it.

Music can be powerful. Music can help you relax. Music can create memories. Music can eliminate fear.

I love N Sync.

When I was a senior in college, they were huge, and so was this show called TRL.

TRL was a pop music countdown show on MTV that played videos. (I'm not going to insert some sort of lame, "OMG, MTV played videos!" joke)

And N Sync's "Bye Bye Bye" was constantly on the charts.

Have you ever heard a song and can't get it out of your head? Bye Bye Bye was mine...for about a year.

I watched the video and thought to myself, "I can do that dance."

So every day, I watched...and I practiced.

I sang to myself. I worked through all the moves. And it was fun.

Now granted, my roommates thought I was a moron. And yes, I pulled the shades before I did this because, I get it...a 22 year old college dude dancing in his own living room to a teenybopper song is kind of weird.

The good thing was...I didn't care.

I was having fun and I was learning something new.

Flash forward another month...

Every year, my college had a mom prom where the senior guys take their moms to a dinner and dance. The senior girls took their dads to a similar one, and then we all met up afterward. It was a send off for the seniors and fun for the families.

About half way through the night, while I was having a conversation with a friend, it happened.

The DJ threw on "Bye Bye Bye."

From across the room, I could see another friend of mine bolting at me. I swear he was jumping over tables, but probably not.

"Bryan, Bryan, you gotta do it."

I knew what "You gotta do it" meant.

So I ran to the dance floor.

And started.

For 3 minutes and 19 seconds, I danced like a madman.

The 500 guys and their moms formed a circle around me, while I went through every sequence and every move. I had zero thoughts in my head...I just did it.

Then it was over.

A couple people came up to me after and said it was awesome. And I'm sure there were a bunch more who thought I was a total tool.

But it didn't matter.

I had fun.

Besides weddings, I had never danced in front of anyone before. And I liked dancing too, so why wouldn't I do it?

It was that fear of being seen and being judged that scared me.

But, I was fine.

People will have their opinions. And that's okay.

And 10 years later, I'm probably the only one who remembers that night anyway.

Everyone is scared at one point or another.

On the golf course, people have fear all the time.

They are scared of hitting the ball in the water, or messing up in front of people, or not showing their true ability.

But with fear, comes the lack of enjoyment.

How do you really know you can like something or be good at something if you're scared of it?

It's okay to fail. It's okay to screw up. It's okay to look like an idiot. It's okay to be wrong.

But at least try. At least give yourself the chance to be good.

Don't let the fear of something new or something different prevent you from showing what you really can do.

If I can dance like a goofball in front of 500 people, then why should I be scared to hit a little white golf ball into a pond? Why should I be scared to really get to know the people I'm playing with? Why should I sacrifice my happiness because I'm scared?

There will always be people in this world that don't think you can do certain things.

But really, it's more about what YOU think you can do.

And it's the people that can eliminate fear and do something different that are the happiest.

Might sound crazy, but it ain't no lie...

Chapter 17

Freak Out and Commitment

I was ready.

I hadn't played all winter and now I was in Florida basking in the sun.

We were teeing it up at The Legends at Orange Lake and what would follow would be the best round of golf of my life....because of one shot.

We started on the 1st hole (shocker!) with condos all around us. I was playing with my dad, my good friend and college roomie, and one of my dad's good friends.

Already, it was fun.

I'm not going to bore you with the shot by shot details even though I remember most of them.

I missed a birdie putt by an inch on the first hole.

Then, craziness happened.

I birdied 7 out of the next 10 holes.

And I even bogeyed the 6th hole. I putted the first one and thought it was in....it peeked in the hole and then rolled all the way back to my feet.

So I had the same 10 foot putt up the hill.

The same thing happened...all the way back to my feet again.

Now, I had a 10 foot bogey putt from the same spot.

I drained that one and moved on.

So, standing on the 12th hole, I was 6 under par.

And I freaked out.

I thought about the course record, telling all my friends about it, and all the stuff that could happen.

Whoops.

Now, I had played enough tournament golf to know that if you get ahead of yourself and start thinking about what could happen, you're in trouble.

Have you ever had a good round going and then think to yourself, "Oh, wow. I just have to bogey the last three holes and I'll have my best round ever."

Then you go double, double, quad.

Yeah, me too.

And I had learned about all the clichéd stuff....take one shot at a time, think positive. All well and good, but nobody really teaches you how to do that.

I bogeyed 12.

Then I parred 13, 14, 15, 16, and 17, but it was a major struggle. I wasn't relaxed and I wasn't comfortable because I was thinking about my score.

Walking up to the 18th hole, I was 5 under.

My roomie unintentionally got into my head.

He said, "There is water on the left over that hill. Aim at the buildings. You don't want to go in the water."

The problem was that's all I heard, "You don't want to go in the water."

Guess where I went?

Splash in the water.

But here's where things were different.

I wasn't mad. I wasn't disappointed. I wasn't frustrated.

I was determined.

I dropped my ball and had a 165 shot all over water to a tiny green.

Everyone in their right mind would have turned slightly right, laid up, got their bogey and signed for a smooth 68.

Glad I'm not in my right mind.

I grabbed my 6-iron out of the bag, took a practice swing, and flushed it to about 15 feet.

It was smooth, it was confident, and it all happened because I did not think about my score one time.

I just made a choice, committed to that choice, and did it.

I wasn't concerned with what the outcome was going to be. I just chose. Sure, I had a target and yes, I wanted to do my best, but I was not thinking about the outcome. I just had a clear vision of what needed to be done.

I walked up to the green and looked at this 15 footer up the hill.

Have you ever had that feeling that no matter what you did, things were going to work out?

I knew that ball was going in the hole.

And it did.

I shot 67 with 2 bogeys and a water ball.

More importantly, I finally stopped focusing on score.

I made a choice based on what was important to me, and was not focused on the outcome.

You know how I preach that Happy Golfers don't keep score?

That round is where it all began.

Chapter 18

You're a Little Slow

One time I danced to the hoedown throwdown.

Yeah, I didn't know what it was either.

Apparently it was the dance from this song that Miley Cyrus did. Not exactly the follow-up I wanted to Bye, Bye, Bye, but nonetheless, it was fun.

And, I didn't do it because I was good. I did it for a girl; a girl who was on the Western Wings Special Olympics golf team.

Every Monday throughout the summer, a group of 20+ athletes from the Special Olympics comes out to practice their driving, chipping, and putting.

They have an area competition and a state competition and they love it.

They play to play.

It's the experience every golfer should have.

So earlier in the evening, she started singing this song. I asked her what she was singing and she said, "The Hoedown Throwdown. You've never heard of it?"

I like to think I know a little bit about pop music, but I had no clue what she was talking about.

"It has a dance too."

Now, she got my attention.

We stopped golfing and she started teaching me this dance. I didn't get it right away, so she let me know.

"You're a little slow."

I just started laughing.

She taught me everything I needed to know about it. And she did it well.

Near the end of class, the athletes gathered together to do the Special Olympics cheer. But we had to do one more thing.

She wanted to do the dance together...in front of the group.

There was no backing out now.

She sang the song while we both went through the moves. She was way better than I was.

The class ended and we said our goodbyes.

Looking back, I realized that day was an ideal golf day for her...and for me.

We were there for an hour. She golfed for about 20 minutes. And she danced and sang for about 40.

She had fun. She laughed and smiled. She had the confidence to entertain the rest of the group. And she'll remember that more than she'll remember a golf shot.

Make sure you get what you want out of your experience.

Play to play.

Chapter 19

The Daddy Caddy

I like games and I like spending time with people.

My grandparents taught me how to play poker when I was 8. My mom was always playing cards at night...she'd play 500 with herself.

In high school, I used to carry around a deck of cards in my pocket. In two of the classes, I'd break out the cards and play. We'd finish our work in calculus and play a little UNO. And in band (yep, band geek!), we'd always have about a half hour of free practice time. We'd "practice" playing cards.

When I turned 18, I was legally allowed in the casinos in Minnesota. So, I did what every 18 year old would do. I went to the casino at midnight when I turned 18, came home and slept for a few hours, went to school, and then went back to a different casino with my dad in the afternoon.

The casino seemed to be our bond. It sounds strange, I know, but it was where we could play together. We brought only what we could afford, and when it was gone, we were done.

Some people see casinos as a waste of money. I see them as a place to play games.

I like competition, but I'm not competitive. I like games, but I don't care if I win or lose.

If it was only about winning and losing, I'd probably be doing something else, because you will definitely lose a lot more than you will win.

But when you play games, you're able to spend more time with people. You can talk, and laugh, and build relationships.

What is it about these games that can improve your experience?

Games teach self confidence, honesty, focus, sportsmanship, responsibility, safety, strategy, concentration, planning, self control, patience, creativity, awareness...the list goes on and on.

Can a casino game or card game teach these things? Maybe not as much as other games, but think about when you were younger...

When I was a little Bryan, one of my favorite things to do was play with the neighbor kids. Every day in the summer, we'd hop on our bikes, and go see who could play that day. Rarely, would there be a day where a group of us wasn't organizing some sort of sports competition.

The day usually worked like this:
Wake up. Play outside. Eat lunch as fast as we could. Go back outside. Play until dark.

As we get older, we have more responsibility, and these days are few and far between. We have commitments and stricter schedules. We try to balance time between family and work. We lose our kid-like instincts, and forget that sometimes, we just need to play.

So a few years ago, I tried to bridge the gap.

Since I teach a lot of families, I wanted something for the families to do together to guarantee all smiles...something that they could do together where everyone could feel like a kid.

So I started The Daddy Caddy.

The Daddy Caddy works like this.......

On a day in late August, kids are invited to play Conviction Creek Chip and Putt course. The kids play 3, 6, or 9 holes depending on age to see who is Champion of the World. Yes, the entire world.

Trophies are boring, so we have a championship belt.

Every player must have a caddy. It doesn't have to be daddy (Daddy Caddy just sounds cool). It can be mom, or grandpa, or Uncle Leo, or a good friend. But, the caddy is necessary. Players cannot carry their own clubs.

There are prizes for everyone. We have giant prize table with a bunch of different things. At the end of the round, the kids simply choose a prize...whatever they like. It does not matter what score they shoot.

And, since I have a sweet tooth, there are some treats too.

The lowest overall score (for the 9-holers 14 and below) will win the Championship Belt. But really, it's not about that at all. It's about spending time with the family, eating a few treats, and having some laughs.

Here's the best part of this whole event. It's free.

My wife will tell you that I turn everything into a game. Not a competition, but a game. Something to play. Something to have a little fun. And something with challenge.

I can learn something from younger Bryan. When you were growing up, it was all about the experience. Sure, some kids would get mad if they didn't win, but you'd all be back out the next day playing again.

The games, the fun, the laughing, the joking, the challenge, the people...that's what mattered.

And that's what still matters.

Chapter 20

The Importance of a Team

Everyone deserves to be part of a team.

Happy people don't do everything themselves. They have people that are willing to help.

That's part of the reason golf can be fun. The team aspect.

I know, you're thinking, golf is an individual sport. Wrong. Nothing is an individual sport. You need people to practice against, people to talk with, people to spend time with, people to play with.

A few years back, we started a team golf program. It was a simple concept. Signup for a team with your friends (or we'll put you on a team), have skills competitions, and play games.

The kids love it.

Why does this work so well?

It includes everyone regardless of skill level.
It focuses on the people part of golf.

It shows kids there is a different way to enjoy something. It makes the experience important.

Last year, one of our teams was playing at a local course.

It started innocently enough.

One kid came up and said, "Can I work for you?"

Before I could even get out an answer, all 12 kids came up and asked me the exact same thing.

I couldn't figure out why.

Then one of my instructors came up to me and whispered in my ear, "I told them that everyone who works for you gets an Iphone."

So I played along.

I asked them why they wanted to work for me.

I got some answers I expected.

"It's fun."
"I love golf."
"You'll buy me an Iphone."

Then one of them said, "I'd love to work for you. All you do is walk around and talk to kids."

I looked at him and said, "That's all you think I do?"

But then I thought about it some more and realized that simple statement kind of sums up what I do.

I walk around and talk to people.

And if you talk with kids, they will tell you everything.

By the end of the first lesson, I know dog names, shoe sizes, dad's job, vacation spots, and the occasional allergy.

It's simple. People get comfortable, they have more fun, they learn more, and they let down their guard. They start to get rid of some fear.

You fear what you don't know. And what you don't know makes you uncomfortable. If you can simply talk to people and ask questions, you start to know.

You understand more about who they are, not just what they do. And you start to have meaningful conversations and relationships.

So, yeah, I walk around and talk to kids...and adults...and whoever else is willing to talk. My hope is that these conversations help people become more comfortable.

But it's not just me who can do this. I have a team.

I would never be successful if it wasn't for the good people around me.

I have my wife who takes care of the family stuff, so I'm able to spread my message.

I have my kids, who keep me grounded, and show me what's really important.

I have friends and family and fans that support what I do.

I have a great friend that I teach with who keeps things organized.

I have a talented group of high school and college kids who want to help kids.

I have a cookie girl, who makes killer cookies for the events.

I have a place to teach with an outstanding leader, who keeps the course and range in great shape.

I have companies that donate things.

I have my dad, who I can bounce ideas off.

The list goes on and on.

Find a team. A team of good people. A team that's willing to help. A team that makes you happier.

There was a girl who started taking lessons from me when she was 7. Short, little blonde girl. She was a dancer and had good balance. And she always smiled. She liked games, she didn't care if she won or lost, and she always came back year after year. She was a decent golfer, but really didn't play that much. She just liked the lessons and occasionally went out to play.

By the time she was 14 or so, golf really wasn't her thing anymore. It was no big deal, but I missed having her in my classes.

Last year, I got an email from her. She was now 19. She wanted to work with me. She wanted to teach kids too. I thought that was awesome that a girl who really didn't play much golf wanted to come teach golf to kids.

Some other pros would look at that and say, "No, I want someone who is good at golf and has played collegiately or professionally."

Not me. I want the people who are fun to be around, who always smile, and who love games.

So, I hired her.

I want people on my team who can walk around and talk to kids.

Who makes your life easier or happier or more fun?

Who helps you?

Who is on your team?

Life is better with a team. Gather yours.

Chapter 21

High School Girls Are People Too

I coach high school girls.

I know what you're thinking, but no, I'm not crazy.

Seven years ago I was giving a lesson to a woman who happened to be the assistant girls' golf coach of a local high school. She asked if I wanted to help out the girls the next season with their swings. It sounded fun, so I considered it.

Later that winter, out of nowhere, the Athletic Director called and asked if I wanted to be the head coach for the girls' varsity team.

I had never coached a high school team before. I didn't know if my teaching schedule would allow it. And to top it all off, I couldn't even talk to high school girls when I was in high school, so how could I do it now?

I took it anyway.

And, I'm glad I did.

Mostly because it opened up a wide variety of players, parents, and friends.

People are what makes this game fun. I've met many good people and hopefully I've coached a few of them to be good people as well.

The Star

The second year I was there, this little 8th grader wanted to play. She was quiet, shy, and putted like she didn't know where the hole was.

But she had two things going for her. She liked golf. And she worked hard.

She worked hard during the season, during the summer, and during the winter. And she liked it.

The following year, as a 9th grader, she played #1 on Varsity, had her career low round, which helped her qualify for the state tournament, and got a hole in one.

But she wasn't done yet.

She qualified for state as a sophomore...and junior...and senior.

I watched her ups and her downs. Her awesome shots and her "what the heck was that?" shots. She talked my ear off, and gave me the silent treatment on the course. I watched her go from a quiet, shy 8th grader to a still quiet, but not so shy college freshman.

Yet, she still has that perfect combination of skill, confidence, and attitude...knowing you're good, proving you're good, but never taking it that seriously.

The best part...now she works with me in the summer giving back to other kids and families.

The Only Rule

I have one rule on my team.

If you're stopping for food before practice, bring me a cookie.

I guess I have two rules.

Real rule: Don't cheat.

It's simple.

If you are playing golf for me, you will not cheat.

If you do cheat, even one time, then you are off the team.

It doesn't matter if you're the number one girl on the team or someone trying to make the team. If I find out you cheated, you're done.

Harsh?

I don't think so...and here's why.

Golf is game that is supposed to be played for fun. Yes, there is competition involved and yes, you want to play your best.

But there's something more important than competition and score...the people you are with.

If you got an 8, take an 8. If the people you are playing with think you got an 8, but you think you got a 7, count again. If you still think you got a 7 and they think you still got an 8, take the 8.

Why?

Because I'd much rather have someone take one more stroke on a scorecard, even if it means losing the match, than have them be known as "the cheater" for the rest of their golfing life.

There are cheaters on almost every team. Those people that try to prove their worth through a score.

Prove your worth through the kind of person you are. Prove your worth through your kindness. Prove your worth by helping others. Prove your worth by creating something enjoyable.

Prove your worth through your character, not your score.

Nobody likes playing with cheaters.

How to Break the Ice

One of the girls on the team once said to me, "Bryan, we're already weird, but you make us weirder."

I'm taking that as a compliment.

I've coached the team for 7 years and we've had our share of characters. We have been decently talented, but not exactly the most motivated bunch in the world.

But the one thing that we have that no other team has...a crazy amount of fun.

We are the team that every other team wants to play with.

Why is that?

We don't take the game that seriously. We talk on the course. We are more concerned about getting to know our playing partners. And we always have food.

One of the little techniques that I taught the girls stemmed from a game my brother and I used to play.

We called it the pop culture game...or the Theo (yes, after Theo Huxtable).

After college my bro and I lived together for a spell. And every morning we'd draw a name out of a giant glass head (don't ask) to reveal what our challenge was for the day.

The names in the head were typically somewhat obscure 80's or 90's pop culture references...Charles in Charge, Steve Urkel, Kris Kross, Joe Piscopo, Vanilla Ice.

Sometime throughout the day, in normal conversation, we had to incorporate what we drew into the conversation.

We did this for a couple reasons.

First, to be different and throw something into a conversation that people may not have heard for a long time. Conversations can be boring, so we wanted to get away from the typical small talk.

Second, we wanted to see if we could make people react to our reference. Bonus points if you got them to laugh.

We were looking for a way we could disarm the person we were talking with. We wanted more than small talk. We wanted real stuff...likes, dislikes, laughter, smiling, hopes, fears, dreams.

So, back to the girls...

It can be nerve-racking or awkward playing with a group of people that you've never met before. And if you're going to be out there for a while with them, you might want to have something to talk about. Better yet, it might be fun to get to know them.

So, every time the girls go out and play with a group, they have a challenge.

The very first time I did this, the challenge was to figure out the other players' middle names.

Simple and not too weird.

Their goal was to do it in a subtle way, even though it didn't always work out that way. On more than one occasion, when they forgot about the challenge, the girls would ask bluntly on the last hole, "Hey, what's your middle name?"

The middle name morphed into favorite ice cream, grandparents' names, shoe size, scariest movie.

Sometimes the goal is just to get them to say a certain word. It is almost like playing 20 questions without the other person knowing you are playing.

Once the girls are able to pick out a small tidbit of information, then the rest is easy. They start to understand more about the person. They ask more questions. They feel comfortable with what they are talking about, and most importantly they get beyond the small talk and have real conversations. It's the Give, Ask, Listen, Laugh, Play method.

Sure, it may not sound like you can have a real conversation about your shoe size, but it just opens doors to other questions. It gets the mind off of golf and focuses on the people involved in the game.

The Writing is on the Ball

Ready for the understatement of the century?

High School girls lose concentration easily.

This is very apparent when some of the girls are playing in matches. They are having fun with their group, then all of a sudden, frustration.

A couple bad shots leads to a bad hole and the girls get frustrated.

The bad hole compounds into losing focus on what's really important. It's a very easy thing to do. Especially when you have to keep score in high school matches.

Before every match I give the girls a golf ball to use. Most of them don't care that much about the ball, so they just toss it in their bag. There's a chance that they use it later if they lose their first one.

During one tournament, the girls needed a morale boost, or a change of focus, so I wrote on their golf balls.

I simply wrote, "Smile" on every ball.

The girls took notice and even though they didn't play better that day, they had more fun.

The next tournament, I wrote on them again.

This time it was more personal for each girl. I based what I wrote on what they liked, their attitude, what they were struggling with, what they thought was funny.

"You are a great putter"
"The sun is out."
"Don't get run over by the lawnmower"

The girls caught on quickly and started focusing on the right things; the things they could control.

Pretty soon, I got requests.

"Write something funny." "Write something only I would get." "Draw something." (Asking me to draw something is like asking me to turn down candy...I don't do it very well)

It became a challenge to write personal and funny things match after match, but it helped me listen more. It helped me ask more questions to the girls. It helped me learn more about them.

I never thought being around a bunch of high school girls could teach me so much. If you focus on the right things…enjoyment, character, and having fun with other people, your experience will be better.

Chapter 22

Clear the Clouds

I lost it.

Besides, "Seriously, you have huge feet" or "Where do you get all your belts?"....that is the phrase I hear most often.

I was playing well, and then I lost it.

And it's not true. (The feet thing is)

You didn't lose your swing. It's still inside of you. It's always been there. There's just something blocking it.

<u>Just because it's cloudy, doesn't mean the sun is gone.</u>

You don't have to create another sun, or make it hotter, or make it shine brighter. You just have to clear away the clouds.

Sometimes the clouds are your attitude. Sometimes the clouds are negative people that are around you. Sometimes the clouds are a crappy day at work or at school. Sometimes the clouds are just some minor distractions.

Your ability is still there. Your happiness is still there. Your kindness, friendship, skill, sense of humor, ability....it's all still there.

In golf, it's my job to figure out what the clouds are. Is it a thunderstorm or is it just partly cloudy? Whatever they may be, they can and will be cleared away.

In the golf swing, the clouds are tension. And this tension starts in the hands.

Most golfers hold on to the club too tightly. Your hands tighten up, then your arms, then your shoulders.....pretty soon you can't even make a somewhat natural swing. The sun is still there, but you have lots and lots of clouds.

I had a woman in class once that said, "Bryan, I was told by another instructor to hold my club like I'm a holding a baby bird. Is that right?'

I told her that's a great analogy. It keeps your hands loose; it allows the club to do its job. Then she interrupted me and said:

"My bird is dead."

Think of how you grip a steering wheel when you drive, think about how you hold your toothbrush or your fork. These are good indicators of how you should be holding the golf club. Unless you are my wife, who makes her gums bleed and her fork cry, then you should be fine.

So, if you want to have more fun and play better...relax your hands.

But most tension is in the mind.

There is the fear of failure, the feeling that you "can't", the feeling that it's too tough.

It's more difficult to clear the clouds in your mind sometimes, but it will happen.

<u>Sometimes it storms for a couple days, but the sun always shines again. The clouds always clear away</u>.

When my mom was diagnosed with lymphoma, throughout her treatment, and when she died, times were tough. Things got cloudy.

But the clouds don't need to stick around. The memories, the good times, the experience, the people...they all help to burn off the clouds and show real light again.

There is happiness somewhere inside every person. Sometimes it takes learning about what makes you happy. Sometimes it takes changing your thoughts. Sometimes it takes clearing the clouds.

Chapter 23

The Next Steps

You read a lot of stories about golf, but hopefully you know now, it's not about golf. The score doesn't matter. The experience matters. Relationships matter. Happiness matters.

So what do you do now?

First:
Embrace perspective

Realize that you have it better than you think you do. There is always some who is in rougher shape than you. So be happy for what you have and remember the good things. Look at things from another point of view. If something bad happens, find the good. Don't be satisfied with one answer or one way of doing something. Take the time to listen to other people and watch how they view situations.

Second:
Choose to be better

It all starts with you. No permission needed. You have what it takes to make yourself happier. You just have to choose to do it. Don't make excuses. Don't complain. Don't put things off. Don't wait. Take an inventory of what scares you, what makes you unhappy, and what you want to change. Go after them. It's only scary because you believe it is. Eliminate your fear. Then, be willing to change.

Third:
Surround yourself with good people

Be friendly, be kind, smile more, help more, love more, care more. Give, ask, listen, laugh, and play. In order to find the good people, you must be the good person. Good people are attracted to other good people.

So you may have to take a look at yourself first. What can I do better? What can I do to make myself happier? What can I do to project a good attitude?

There will always be distractions. There will always be setbacks. I still work hard every day on everything that matters to me.

But you know that you are better than those distractions. You know that it could be just a simple choice or a simple sacrifice and your world will become happier.

Do it now.

You can be happier. You will be happier.

My mom would always say, "Every day is a birthday."

Go have a happy one.

For more information on Bryan, his golf academy, and his seriously cute kids, visit

www.bryansgolf.com

www.thehappiestgolfer.com